Rough Draft

Tori Barney

BookLeaf Publishing

India | USA | UK

Presentation by *BookLeaf Publishing*

Web: www.bookleafpub.com

E-mail: info@bookleafpub.com

ISBN: 9789360944445

First edition 2024

To my found family for always supporting me

ACKNOWLEDGEMENT

Thank you to Connor and Genna for all the help.

PREFACE

Because a twenty-one day writing challenge was the motivation I needed to stop procrastinating my passion.

The First of Friends

I was never more myself
then when I was scream singing in the car with
you to remixes of our favorite 2000's pop songs.

I was never more myself
then I was when we were on Facebook chat
creating cheat sheets for all the emoticon
combinations.

I was never more myself
then I was when we would recall old inside
jokes that never made any sense
but continues to kill us and connect us till death.

I was never more myself
then I was with you staying up, sharing secrets
at sleepovers
and when we'd turn over to finally say
goodnight
someone's sleeping bag would make a fart noise,
erupting a roar of laughter
causing the whole process to start all over.

My first everythings
were with you.

You were the first place
first face
that ever felt safe.

The Perfect Day

A cold rainy day
with animated movies
reading a good book

You & Me

It all started with a
Little Red Car.
A paper town node
on a map of our own.
Everything in that space with you felt
different.
Maybe it was the gentle glowing fluorescent
lights of the road.
Maybe it was the soft hum of the singing engine.
And as late as it was, I don't remember ever
feeling that awake.
I'd listen to you talk, drinking in your words,
watching your pupils expand.
While mine squinted real small from smiling so
hard.
A space that was safe.
Where words could exist in thin air. Ideas to
grow.

Until the invisible shift.
An impossible journey that you wanted to take
somebody else on.
Fighting for you was like fighting to get from
Oklahoma to Mexico, and I was Texas.

You avoided me altogether.
That Little Red Car that once made my heart
beat of joy,
now made my heart beat stop all at once.
I never knew like that a connotation could twist.
but now all I wish
is to forget that space would ever exist.

The Escape Breaker

I dreamed of a way to get out.
To leave behind the enormous weight of
permanent markers, created by imaginary
monsters.
I would bury the truth beneath the water.
And if people asked me where I was from, I
would tell them what I wanted them to believe.
Studying abroad gave me an
unexpected,
unfamiliar
comfort, sculpted through the differences of
others.
Mahogany skies
and the soft misty air
make the possibilities and experiences seem
endless.
like something in a book
The Book of the Living
I will forever be grateful to have lived part of
my life being another version of myself.
The one I was maybe too afraid to be in my
current location.
Because perspective can sometimes be
everything.

That make or break, when we just need a place to
Escape.

A Lone Home

I won't let broken dishes and worn out hinges
define me.
I won't let tarnish relations and abusive
positions define me.
They ask,
"Why can't we go to your house?"
"Why can't we meet your mom?"
It's because then my friends will know why the
old ones don't talk to me anymore.
She separates the feeling, maybe because of the
sad.
You can draw a line in the sand, but that doesn't
make you become any better of a man.
My brother and I hide
Who we are
and what we do.
No family to exist, but the blood of our own.
We create borders and boundaries.
We learn a million new names in order to forget
an old one.
We try to forget the past
and pray for a better future.
One where we aren't the only ones looking out
for each other.
From place to place

without leaving a trace.
Forever Feeling Alone
because at the end of the day we all know a
house doesn't make

I Find Comfort in the Comments of Truce

I Find Comfort in the Comments of Truce
music on the surface
behind is hope
He tells us to stay
They are proud of me
They are listening to me in the night
28 million friends
They keep me company
I'm never alone
"You're here."
"You did it."
"You can keep going."
even if you think you can't
They know you can
We're all here for the truce project
tonight no one will be a prisoner

Don't Chase the Light

I miss people that cease to exist past my finger
tips.
There's not enough room left for me anymore.
Do they ever miss the parts of me I've stolen
from them?

F. HA

chaine turns to modern love on the sidewalk
retelling the story of how we take over the black
and white world
play fighting in the park
the awkwardness of adult life
searching for your person across the room
finding out what you're supposed to do
when you're supposed to do it

February 3rd

You are the most beautiful
copy and paste
of a life I wish I was lucky enough to
experience.

I watch him watch the stars.
Some things never change.
Some things are so familiar
like the greatest pieces of my past are
intertwined with the potential of my future.

I Want to Be

I want to be nothing.
I want the forgotten text.
The reassurance of someone always being better
The emotionless touch.
The water streaming home.
The reflection of crescents.
The wrist grab when he's pissed, to normalize
the falling.

I want to be everything.
I want to live in the summer,
to infinitely pretend.
To forever be my rising
when I know I'll only ever be my moon.
I want to dance on white lines
instead of making them.
To breathe without drowning.
To fly in addition to falling.

I just want me, all the time,
but I think she got lost along the way
damaged by the mess.

How are You Really?

"How are you?"
The lady behind the register
scoots and scans my items.
She bags my fruity cereal and 2% milk
while I ponder the question.
How am I?
Does she actually want to know?

I'm tired.
No.
I'm exhausted.
Physically. Mentally. Emotionally.
My very soul, weary.

Do I tell her how my only TV remote has been
missing all week?
Do I also then tell her how my dog was the one
that decided to eat it?
And then how do I even begin to explain the
story of how he even managed to do that.
So now I have medical bills swallowing me in a
sea of stress and in an attempt to feel better I go
to my comfort food.
Fruity Pebbles

But unfortunately as I'm pouring my milk it's
more like a soupy pudding.
Which brings me here.
Here in hopes to bring some kind of light at the
end of this dark demon tunnel.
And on the way to here my car tries to cheer me
up by flashing its big bright check engine light.
Surprise!
I pull into the parking lot shrugging off the
sadness.
I'm here for my fruity goods that will make
everything better.

And that's when it happens.

Making my way through the lot I stub my little
pinky toe on someone's cart they left out in the
open.
I go down hard.
The tears well up in my eyes just thinking about
it again.

How am I really?
"I'm good." I smile at her.

She is

She is pretty like city lights.
She sparkles and shines.
A glitter of hope in a world of dark

She is strong like thunder
bound to boom.
No one with more passion
No one more intense

She is soft like summer rain.
A slight pitter patter on the window
curled up in a different world
in the safety of your bed.

Her laugh is like lilacs
sweet and innocent
its contagiousness blossoms to others

She is a scrapbook
full of memories
love and laughter
rolled into one.

I Find Comfort in the Comments of My Blood

I find comfort in the comments of my blood
a shared song
between broken hearts
a song played at too many funerals
for brothers and sisters
that should still be here
but at least we aren't alone
we can continue with kindness
to each other
to ourselves
Te acompaño en el sentimiento

Questions Asked as a Server

What is the difference between the 6oz sirloin
and the 8oz sirloin?
Is there bacon on the bacon burger?
Can I get my salmon cooked medium rare?
How many chicken tenders come with the three
piece chicken tenders?
Can I get you to-go?
Which one is the blackberry lemonade and
which one is the mango?
Do you accept Bitcoin?
Are the chicken wings vegan?
We know you close in ten minutes but can we
still get a table?
Can you please sing even though it's technically
not their birthday?
How much is a water?
Can I have the cheese quesadilla with no cheese
on it?

Still

heard it on the FM
dancing in the PM
those late nights when the headlights were the
view
screaming songs with your best friends
invincible at best
existing in the mess
you trade collections of tomorrow
for the smile of today
nothing in the world could make you
regret it
forget it
you're as magic as the mirrors
reflecting the light of your soul
lavender lullabies will soon slip you to
tomorrow
but tonight
stay for awhile

The City

back in Chicago
forever people watching
becoming myself

Vanilla

I want to get lost in you.
I want to find you in everyday spaces,
in the words within the pages.
I want you to get lost in me.
Because when you see me,
finally see myself.
It's those cheesy movies, you already know the
plot,
but still dying to see how it ends.
It's those late night conversations
that make the moon magic.
I drink in your words for hours.
I think.
I believe.
I could do this forever.

What Good is Sorry?

What good is sorry
when promises become empty?
When you put on a mask of lies and smile for
the sake of it
It shines through
That unforgivable
unforgettable
Shade of black
When your actions never quite match your
words
Even if intent isn't ill
When oceans overflow with emotion
When the light is already out
The door already closed
The sky is just a storm

What good is sorry
when you're done?
You have been
You wish things were different

They aren't
and for that
you're sorry.

When in Rome

cooking class chaos
The Colosseum vomit
tall and fluffy trees

Noise

Black
endless darkness
endless space
drifting on over and over and

Brown
on the silent highway late at night
the warm glow of lights flicker across your face
in the backseat
once you've pulled off you close your eyes and
guess with each turn how close you are to home

Red
a hidden waterfall
one you can only find on accident
tucked between rocks and tangled vine
A spontaneous surprise

Orange
an overnight flight to anywhere
everyone has finished eating
the stewardess turns off the light
the only glow that remains is the occasional
screens here and there
small whispers mix with the sound of sleep

Yellow
the pale cream goes on for miles
as the wind pushes particles around
it's hard to see
it's hard to breathe
Will we ever be found?

Green
a million raindrops splatter onto
a million waxy tree leaves
the kind of heavy rain that makes you look up at
the sky and just accept it
born again

Blue
ominous thunder rumbles and rolls its way in the
distance
blankets are pulled up over noses
the glow of the TV reflected on our faces
a summer storm

Purple
most people want the world to sleep
but others need the noise to breathe
the cars swifty swish pass each other
the trains mimic the soft sound of falling rain
it reminds us that the night continues on
and tomorrow will always come

Pink
Mcdonald's sprite
crisp and crunchy
and most of all spicy

Grey
the black and white lines squiggle together on
the screen
nothing left to distract you from the overthinking

White
the box fan spins from the next room
even at the darkest part of the day there will
never be enough
the type of summer when even the shorts and
sheets are too hot

An Ode to My Brother

I remember watching The Little Mermaid eating
mandarin oranges and
pretending to eat them like Ursula eats the
shrimp.
I remember camping for concerts at 4am for our
favorite bands.
I remember our dance duets.
I remember spinning steering wheels.
I remember having sleepovers in each other's
rooms because it was cooler than being in our
own.
I remember bribing each other with snacks so
we'd never have to go to the store alone.
I remember green apple and blue raspberry ice
cream on the bike trail.
I remember the way you cross your legs when
you sleep
like you're sitting at a talk show interview.
I remember Barbie movies and dancing in the
living room.
I remember that thing with the rainbow at Six
Flags.
I remember it all.
Thank you for giving me so many memories to
remember.